Galia Carolina is a Colombian-born sociologist, writer, and artist now living in London with her British husband and their daughter. She focuses her artistic and literary skills on the difficult topic of eating disorders. Using surrealism, she brings to life the human experiences of those suffering from anorexia, bulimia, and other food-related disorders. She works with professionals in the field on outreach, education, and prevention. In October 2022, she presented two murals of her charcoal drawings at the Hispanic American Conference on Eating Disorders in Monterrey, Mexico. She is currently working on a series of oil paintings depicting children with 'food on their mind.'

To my daughter, it was never your fault!

Galia Carolina Smith

WHY MY DAUGHTER? FROM BINGE EATING TO RESTRICTION

An Intergenerational Journey to the Epicentre of an Eating Disorder

AUSTIN MACAULEY PUBLISHERS™

LONDON · CAMBRIDGE · NEW YORK · SHARJAH

A CIP catalogue record for this title is available from the British Library.

ISBN 9781035826711 (Paperback)
ISBN 9781035826728 (ePub e-book)

www.austinmacauley.com

First Published 2024
Austin Macauley Publishers Ltd®
1 Canada Square
Canary Wharf
London
E14 5AA

This book arose from a process and a hunger to understand the reality behind an eating disorder diagnosis.

This affair of almost 10 years of inquiries within my husband's family and mine, added to the observations of how the disease presented itself and evolved in my daughter, catapulted me to understand – apart from all written material – the context, the environment, and possible triggers for the disease.

My gratitude extends to many people here in England, in Colombia, my country of origin, and to the families here mentioned – actors and actresses in this plot – Everyone has been part of this process. Their stories, perspectives, and knowledge have been filling the impertinent and empty vessels of my understanding. I am grateful to all of them for the attention, dedication, and time they gave me when sharing their narrations.

To my husband – and father of my daughter – in England, and to my deceased father, I owe much and appreciate both their generosity of sharing and giving of oneself, knowing how to wish the best, that selfless and unconditional love for my daughter.

Above all, my thanks are extended to my beloved daughter. In her I see the generations included in this book – parents, grandparents, and great-grandparents – who somehow are still alive and are part of the plot that has triggered an eating disorder in her.

Her struggle to survive has inspired the publication of this book. It is to her that I am mainly grateful for what she has taught me, what she has awakened in me, and the way in which she has strengthened me to understand the complexity of this deadly disease that increasingly plagues the younger generations of our planet.

Darling, your bravery, your determination, and courage have lit the way to these few lines and drawings.

London 2024

Table of Contents

An Intergenerational Journey to the Epicentre of an Eating Disorder (ED) [1]

It was never your fault
January 2023

---

[1] For the sake of clarity, I will refer here to EDs (Eating Disorders) as a set of abnormal eating behaviours; obsession with weight regulation, distorted attitudes and perceptions about body weight and shape (MacNeill, et al., 2017).

List of Drawings

Introduction

As I look out of the window onto the street from our flat in London, England, I suddenly remember my now twenty-year-old daughter was diagnosed with an eating disorder (ED) eight years ago this very week.

I can hardly believe that she managed to escape anxiety-induced overeating as a pre-teen, passing through bulimia and then a purging anorexia, the cause of her long-standing debilitating condition. This pendulum swing from one extreme to the other, from **overeating** (or binge eating) to **restriction** (anorexia) has persistently caught my attention. Why did it manifest itself in this way? The answers elude me.

But I have also had the strength to persevere and patiently love this journey that we as a family have ahead of us, for my daughter, for my home, for myself, and also for you, as you read this book! Strength and patience are part of recovery. And when we work through things together, we can overcome any odds.

I get choked up just sharing that I see only a trivial improvement thus far, but it's gradual and sustained because she's so resilient and committed to her own health. With this entry, I certainly am not implying a full recovery (there is no need to declare victories so hastily); but rather progress in terms of her somewhat more stable mental and physical health: my daughter can enjoy more peaceful meals; her anxiety has decreased significantly, and this gave room for wider mental spaces and congruent levels of awareness. Her weight, body mass, muscle and fat levels are no longer *well below* the healthy limit, yet remain low; together, self-destructive behaviours, depressive episodes, crises, and the obsessive part of the ED are less prominent. By and large, we see a horizon of achieving goals that are self-determined, health-oriented and autonomous. In other words, a physical and mental connection to her essence is gradually emerging.

Beneath all this sharing, there flows a yearning to communicate an **absolutely** necessary progression of *understanding*. Of *decanting*. Tapping the precious liquid of truth about this condition, where the easiest thing to do at times can be to fly off the handle and aggravate its vile and harmful aspects. I am no specialised ED healthcare professional, and these pages contain no scientific claims whatsoever. I am only a companion, a witness, an apprentice, an artist; but above all, I am a mother. My drive to publish these insights about life simply stems from the countless times I suffered with a longing to understand: What sort of environment feeds into developing an ED? Whether right or wrong, I have always believed that the answer to this question holds important keys to treatment and prevention.

And, of course, even the clues that seem most mysterious and impossible to understand also begin to reveal themselves in the midst of the process. Like the question I never stop asking myself, and perhaps the reason that brings us both here: ***Why did this happen to my daughter?***

Behind the curtains of my narrative, there are the actors and sources of information that have given rise to a real-life plot, with real flesh-and-blood characters. I should begin by acknowledging the entire team involved in my daughter's treatment (psychologists, psychiatrists, general practitioners and nutritionists, to name just a few). They all played a decisive role and proved to be instrumental in the mission to save and rescue my daughter from the jaws of death over the past eight years. I single them out because, by the sheer force of working with them for so long, I have become imbued with their dedication and commitment to the lives of young people fighting this lethal disease, and the conviction necessary to share this story.

My own close experience with ED has been a very reliable and trustworthy source of information; as the sole caregiver of my daughter at home for three years, I dedicated myself to the challenge of learning more and more about this crippling and deadly condition, which, as it happens, has become widespread in our days. While we may be a small family (father, mother and daughter) that has dealt with great difficulties, we have also developed powerful strengths. One is the commitment to **self-awareness**, a resource of tremendous importance to our lives in recent years. The constant self and family exploration prompted me to delve deeper into our ancestors, my daughter's grandparents and great-grandparents, to better understand their relationships with their bodies and food. This *logbook* contains every tough question I ventured to ask and the blunt answers I received from relatives over the past decade. While many of them are no longer with us, I am still grateful for their transparency and insightful sharing. This enquiry includes open and honest conversations with my daughter and husband, how he and I have dealt with issues of the body and food since childhood, and how our understanding and experience of that relationship may have led to ED in our home. I could hardly overlook my daughter's background from my own pregnancy, including her childhood through to the development of the disease itself, or the personality and environmental factors whose impact contributed to the onset of ED.

Oddly enough, a careful study of my own work as a caregiver was also helpful. Not because I do it right or wrong, but because it keeps me always ready to know myself better, to recognise all my weaknesses and not to confuse my path with hers. This "observer" project has certainly exposed all my mistakes, shortcomings and limitations. In the last eight years, with the best intentions of helping my daughter, I have made many mistakes, I have gone too far, I have blocked her process, I have lashed out against her and against the disease, ignoring that it was not my place to do such a thing. I have said the wrong thing, thought the wrong thing and acted without thinking. I have walked a narrow path to do what my daughter required of me, even if it was not what I wanted to do, where a fine and subtle line stood between everything. But I have learnt to resist there, without straying from that line, for as long as I can; it is a slow but steady walk. I have been calmly writing my feelings and thoughts from this "fine line". I have even opened my mind to things that are beyond my understanding (which is a lot), admitting their importance, expressing it openly, and this has also served my daughter well.

Certainly, my words leave aside the filters of what others will say. I have lived with them for a long time and they no longer matter. Who am I pleasing when I hide what **it is**? By pretending to live a life of perfection, telling fairy tales, I am only fooling myself, with this fantastic premise that *I am in control*. There is no such thing as a standard, objective and unbiased public opinion that can be pleased and controlled. The collective subject referred to as the *masses* is also a fictitious point of reference to understand what's normal social behaviour. Reality hurts neither acquaintances nor strangers. On the other hand, when we try to "polish" this reality by accommodating the "discourse" to keep up appearances, we bleed and betray our inner selves, our children and the family unit. The difficulty with *what people will say* is that it overlooks reality: we all speak, judge, and condemn; that is human nature. However, human nature equally gained an understanding of compassion, devotion, sincere and genuine communication, love and true sacrifice for others.

"Stripped bare", I can and want to see what went wrong, unashamedly, boldly and with an open mind to admit my ignorance and acknowledge that yes, there are answers; even if it hurts to open up that palette of possibilities, I throw myself into the void of honesty.

While my husband and I have a family background that may not shine brightly as an ancestral dynasty, and in many ways they have been wonderful, they have also had a hand in the disease for a variety of reasons, including their own suffering and painful experiences in the past. Please note that my enquiry is not about examining all the good or positive things that families can do to support a boy or girl with an ED. I am nevertheless aware that the family, the relational space where the very fabric of society is interwoven, constitutes a

17

vital support and sustenance during rehabilitation. A loving and caring family commitment to caring for the affected child is indispensable and necessary. I will however try to focus these pages only on how the family, unintentionally and unconsciously, can become harmful—and even perversely twisted—influencing the outcome when a vulnerable child is affected by the disease. In addition to providing an effective toolkit, I hope these reflections will help raise awareness and understanding of this struggle, so that we can prevent further misfortune and doom among the young people of today, and those of tomorrow.

This account is not intended to be a systemic and exhaustive academic approach. I am aware of the many additional factors not addressed here, such as recent research in the field of neurobiology, genetics, etc., findings that are pivotal to a thorough study of the origins of ED in young people. My study is an approach that focuses on intergenerational factors, family context and personality traits that may have colluded in the development of the disease. Our family's story is just one of many examples of what can happen behind closed doors in any household dealing with a mental health challenge.

I am sharing a pendulum-like intergenerational and family movement over time: from abundance to scarcity, from binge eating to restriction, from wastefulness to stinginess. Extending beyond eating, this dynamic likewise affects body care, personal finances, academic performance and affective-emotional areas. While this pendular swing per se does not necessarily constitute a decisive factor in the illness, I have learned that our family has always had a psychic balancing equation (understood as the search for equilibrium or counterbalance) replicated at the individual, family and intergenerational levels, with the corresponding risks and consequences. While everything written here is true—and I've strived to be truthful—it is still only my truth, my experience and my subjective, partial, fallible and debatable point of view. For the sake of objectivity, I have opted to change or modify the names of the people in this story to protect their identities, but I must point out that they all existed and are real.

I
It's Personal
A Family and
Intergenerational Matter

In telling the story of why ED entered our home, I hope to avoid raising false expectations or promising that you will find definitive conclusions or correlations here. I am also unable to give advice or recommendations to anyone reading this who is also going through something similar. The ultimate aim of this story is to *share* our story. I am, however, absolutely certain that peering into our generational history deepened our personal and family understanding of my daughter's ED. Moreover, we have been able to surmise that our original families, and we the parents, were already exhibiting a disordered and quite possibly pathological pattern of eating behaviours when she was diagnosed with ED. We just hadn't noticed it. This realisation had a significant impact, because it highlighted the need for a systematic adjustment of all our family eating behaviours. More importantly, it became a vital guide in helping us learn how to care for our daughter in her treatment with a view to dismantling the disease, but it also convinced us to begin our own recovery.

There are certainly additional factors that also contributed significantly to our daughter's marked improvement in recent years. I say factors in plural because not just one definitive element, but many, have served and continue to serve: namely, her commitment to psychological therapies, and the many books that have instructed us as the disease develops. Sincerity and honesty within the family unit on a daily basis has been another key component, a scenario that encourages trust as my daughter grows in stature, knowledge and maturity, and as we grow in experience and age. Naturally, not every family will find the same factors equally valuable. Every young person is an entirely different universe, every family has its own method of dealing with its challenges, and every generational line bears a world full of its own information, context and biography. From our journey as caregivers, we have learned that there is no need to create a "special bubble" at home, apart from an atmosphere of mutual trust and normal communication, with the minimum standards of care that any family strives for in this century. I believe that all these variables mentioned as contributing to improvement were and continue to be aligned with recovery, always aiming to save lives.

With these words, my wish is to share humanity. Perhaps a mother like me, or even a father learning to care for his or her child in the midst of this scourge, will find much more.

As a witness and companion, I can vouch that this intergenerational, family and contextual journey has opened the door that led me to a discovery: the pieces do fit together.

A – I draw what I see without any shame.

I wanted to put my experience down on paper, not only in writing but also in pictures, as I cannot always find the words to process what happened. The strength of the drawing comes from the idea that consciousness is mediated and transformed through form and symbols. I consider that the images themselves, my drawings, have been equally valuable instruments, equally insightful in unveiling this plot.

When I paint or draw, I inevitably sit down to observe, feel and think. The drawing holds and contains my overflowing emotions: it orders, clarifies, names, accepts and even frames them. In addition, my task of drawing what I see and how I see it has helped me digest the harrowing experience of accompanying my daughter through her recovery. The experience was tormenting because it opened my eyes to her agony and revealed how ED had a stranglehold on her. By directing my gaze towards our ancestors, drawing also enabled me to confront myself, my illness, and I was able to see the world around me without any filters or reservations.

While I agree that the very act of drawing is cathartic, I am more inclined to believe that a finished drawing can prove beneficial to others, rather than only remaining at the service of the person who made it. For me, in a sense, drawing has a life of its own. The drawings want to go out to convey messages and answers that language does not always have. Through drawing and meditating, I have also been able to write down what I have learned. These written words are my bridge of contact, the garment of my emotions; the drawings are the vast landscape, without horizon, without beginning or end. The inexhaustible source of psychic energy of presence, identity and essence itself is my whole being.

II

I Cannot See You in the Present, So I Seek You in the Past

The first time I drew my daughter going through an ED, I depicted her back to me; although she was there with me, I couldn't see her face. I chose to draw her inverted from the waist upwards, with her torso facing the other way round, and thus found my own way of interpreting the ED. That was my definition of the disease. Unusual, perhaps, but the drawing explained it to me. That's really how I saw it. As if she were all there, her body, her mind, her spirit, all her components present in a single image; I was looking for her, her essence, but I could not find her, and she was not aware of my existence

Drawing 1: *I Can't See You, 2022.*

either. Something in it read uninhabited, empty, vacant. My daughter was not in her place as she used to be. Her appearance, her profile, betrayed her absence. Parts of her behaviour, her thinking revealed something else. The disease had overshadowed her life. Although she turned her face to look at me, I felt as if she still had her back turned, as if she had turned her back on life. However, it was not an absolute surrender. There was no doubt that a substantial part of my daughter, her *essence*, was struggling to hang on to her living space.

To change the course of a path, it is essential to know how one arrived there; the frame, the colours of the painting, the landscape, the sketch of the drawing; its background! Every therapist would eventually ask my husband and I the same question: What factors do you think may have combined to lead to this course of your daughter's illness? At the beginning we always answered: Nothing! We are an ordinary family with no dietary, physical or genetic abnormalities that might have triggered this disease. To our surprise, the psychiatrist who had been seeing my daughter for some time ruled that my daughter met *all* the requirements, the "raw material" necessary to get the disease. At my astonishment and insistence, the specialist generously explained and answered all our questions, concluding that my daughter had always been a "time bomb".

Looking closely at the full picture that produced such a strong conclusion, my attention was drawn to the eating behaviour patterns of my family and my husband's family. I therefore set out to explore and inform myself, without filters or value judgements.

All of a sudden, I saw something.

I noticed that my familiarity with risk behaviours associated with eating disorders went beyond the fact that I was a caregiving mother. Even if they never developed in the past, ED triggers have been around in my family environment for at least the past three generations, though with different identities, manifestations and effects in the lives of the people who suffered from them. The first element I identified was an environment of food restriction.

Eusebio, my Colombian father of indigenous descent, the son of farmers in the eastern Andes and a tireless worker, only ate when he felt he deserved it, saying: "Today I have earned my food". He could go for hours without food, especially on days when his business was not making money. In his mind, the day he did not "produce" he did not eat, for he had not earned that right, even if he had the money to buy food. All his energy was spent on doing, being productive, and thus generating resources to avoid the poverty and hunger he experienced in his childhood, when he became an orphan. A number of years later he was diagnosed with stomach cancer. The combination of gastritis and chronic ulcers throughout his life, coupled with his alcohol intake, may well have been the executioner that ended his time in this world. His motto "work, work, work" kept him always on the move, with an infectious hyperactivity and energy, an overwhelming charisma, and an exceptionally good sense of humour. Many people remember him as a true father for his care, magnanimity, empathy and consideration for the suffering of others. I think Eusebio spent his life trying to alleviate the pain of others with devotion, affection and charitable gifts, while numbing his own pain with alcohol.

At the other end of the spectrum, Rosa Isabel, my mother, whom I remember as obsessed with a diet that proclaimed nutrition and wellness but that, far from promoting health, focused on beauty and the need to be in control. Her foray as a student at the local beauty and aesthetics centre, along with her experience as a runaway model, built up a following of admirers wherever she went. Shortly after the birth of her first two daughters, she set up a beauty salon at home. Her obsession with beauty and comfort merged, fostering an environment of body worship, with implications for everyone in the family. Several years later, she was diagnosed with overhydration (potomania) as a result of her excessive intake of water to hydrate her body and skin, a condition that led to coma due to dissolved sodium levels in her brain chemistry.

I can understand her rigorous body care when I see the other side of the coin, a mirror in which Mum didn't want to look: her own mother's carelessness. My mother tells me that Grandma Sofia was an incredibly beautiful woman in her youth, but after having fourteen children, four of whom died in infancy, she neglected her physical appearance to such an extent that she hid from her own family and friends. After losing all her teeth, with neither alternatives nor any will for treatment to restore her dental health and self-esteem, she spent her remaining days as a recluse.

I remember Grandma Sofia as someone with a great disdain for cooking, for men, for her husband and for her own life. Her most recurrent expression: Damned gobbler of mine! She lived with stomach distension, hid food and went for hours without eating. When I was little, she would confess to me how worried she was about how heavy her coffin would be. This was why she restricted her food intake until that dreaded hour.

My mother's father Andrés (and Sofia's husband) was a city man, born in the capital, intelligent, refined, an inventor and silent. He had a great passion for tango. Despite being an elegantly dressed intellectual, his self-esteem was in tatters. As the illegitimate son of a wealthy local landowner, he had to live in hiding all his life, cloistered in his mechanic's shop, never boasting or bragging. He lived in the basement of the house with a fixed idea of not deserving anything. He had bought a lottery ticket with the winning number, and they had to ring him up to claim the million-dollar prize; all he had to do was present the ticket. He searched endlessly, but never figured out where he had put it. Perhaps what he was looking for deep down was his own worth, and not finding it, he could not claim his true fortune. My grandma used to say that she had married a "miserable, poor, good-for-nothing".

Grandma Sofia may have had delusions of grandeur because of her European, and more precisely Scandinavian, roots and the luxuries she lived with her privileged father, but all of that evaporated when her own mother died. Her stepmother cruelly dumped her in a distinguished convent for nuns. It was there that she secretly met Juan, the love of her life, whom she never married. When the time came for her to decide, she hurriedly married my grandfather Andrés—as she would later tell me—only because she had promised herself to marry "the first fool who proposed to me, no matter who it was". Sofia was heartbroken, bitter and haunted by the betrayal of her best friend, who ended up marrying Juan.

Sofía and Andrés led a life full of cover-ups and secrets, apparently because my grandfather had witnessed a murder. Threats forced them to escape to an undisclosed village in Colombia and live in total anonymity. Her children remember her as always ill-tempered, nagging and somewhat manipulative. She was, however, industrious, hard-working, an activist and also the breadwinner in the family.

Andres, for his part, lived away from home, downstairs in a small, isolated and lonely cubicle. Increasingly withdrawn, he took on small mechanic jobs to provide something for the household, but his hobby was designing vehicles for the future, flying saucers, prefabricated houses and similar inventions, all in pencil and all with prodigious detail. He dreamt of intergalactic travel, spoke of astronauts and dwellings as far away as they were beautiful, yet also affordable for everyone. At the time, his ideas seemed ridiculous and fanciful to many, especially his wife.

Both were inmates in the penitentiary of resignation, conformism, disillusionment and deprivation. This life of "mental arrest" became evident to me for Grandma Sofia, who showed a slightly perverse fascination with caged animals; she kept birds, squirrels, parrots, all in small cages, confined in a tiny courtyard. Dozens of them were noisy and all were rather neglected. She only liked animals that sang, made noise, and did *something* for their food; the ones that worked and entertained her! She would give them chocolate soup with bread, each in turn.

Regarding human food, the daily scene was chaotic. The pots emerged from the kitchen and were set on the table for the main meal at midday. This would unleash a struggle amongst the ten siblings for control over the trays. Sometimes the older siblings, emboldened by their own frenzy, by the absence of discipline and basic boundaries, would grab the whole pot and run off with it, leaving the rest without lunch. Although Sofia had workers at home to help her, she could not cope. She ran a restaurant all on her own and made a little extra by charging nightly parking fees to tractor-trailer and lorry drivers hauling food to the capital. Their home, paradoxically, was huge, and the garage accommodated such a parking service.

Sophia instituted a system in her household whereby the daughters (five) served the sons. The painful experience of losing her mother, how her stepmother and the nuns treated her, and also her best friend's betrayal might have turned her against women. She told me women always betray their friends *because they were women*.

As I glance around Sofia and Andres' home, I can clearly see that, while the atmosphere was dominated by an abundance of food—in the restaurant and also the lorries parked at home—the very epicentre of the household lived in total austerity. A mentality of deprivation and selfishness prevailed, depicted in how the eldest sons hoarded the food served. The siblings lived in an environment full of animosity, suspicion, bullying and competition. The older boys demanded attention and services from their sisters. The sisters were jealous and envious of each other. While the boys attended public schools, and each of the five had their own room, the girls shared a single room and took turns wearing the few school uniforms they had at home, so that one would always get a warning from the school.

As for my grandparents on my father Eusebio's side, there is only the emptiness of not having known them. They are known to have been farmers in a very fertile region of Colombia, a former indigenous reservation. Because Eusebio, the youngest of four siblings, lost his mother at the age of two and his father shortly thereafter, he was left under the precarious supervision of his older siblings, who were in no position to help him. His two older sisters withdrew to the local convent, leaving Eusebio even more lonely, unprotected and vulnerable. Eusebio recalled sleeping, in his own words, in a "thousand-star hotel" (the municipal park), until a passer-by noticed and gave him food and shelter for a while.

Eusebio and Rosa Isabel both developed reactive behaviours in response to the deprivations they experienced during childhood. The lack of the basic resources for survival, such as food, care, acceptance and affection, fuelled Eusebio's insatiable desire to have, to possess and to see abundance. As for Rosa Isabel, she came from an environment of secrecy and deprivation, shaped by a belief that *she didn't deserve anything*, that *she wasn't good enough*, and that being shy was almost a virtue. Although she grew up in total austerity, she always longed for the comfort and wellbeing that her own mother, my grandmother Sofia, so desperately wanted. Against this backdrop, Eusebio plunged himself into earning money, training and working tirelessly, sometimes doing two or more jobs at the same time. He ultimately committed himself to a single pursuit: *to accumulate more and more*.

In Rosa Isabel's sizeable family, Eusebio found an answer to his questions about what his own family should be like. Initially attracted by her sister, he showed up at Sofia's house with presents, sweets and boundless charisma. I don't know how, but Rosa Isabel ended up pregnant by Eusebio at the age of 18, and they married soon after.

Rosa Isabel had a great longing to be admired, she wanted to leave behind poverty, servility to her male siblings, contempt, envy, and life "in a crowd". She naturally fantasised about being able to take care of herself, eat and dress well. When she discovered that Eusebio was a man with ambition ("*echado p'adelante*" as they say where I come from), his generosity, affection for everyone in his house and his ability to make a living, she spotted a promising future husband.

After getting married, Rosa Isabel and Eusebio went to live in the house of Sofía and Andrés, where their first daughter was born. Eusebio focused on training, working from dawn to dusk until he could afford to put down a deposit on a house. They left there with two young daughters, ready to settle in the capital, leaving behind the family of origin and establishing their own.

The austerity that marked the lives of our ancestors seemed to trigger a latent tendency to live "at the extremes", as if it were the norm. This polarity permeated the ensuing generations, my life and the lives of my siblings. Eusebio provided for his children's basic needs throughout their lives; food, shelter, education and housing. Years later, he even financially supported Sofía and Andres' entire household, providing them with food, jobs, cars, and, if that wasn't enough, all his love.

Eusebio and Rosa Isabel always wanted something better. It was an unstoppable fire raging in both of them and holding them together. Their constant changes of house in search of a better house, a school, a car, were erasing the traces of poverty

31

in the minds of Eusebio and Rosa Isabel. Squandering soon came knocking, as a home with fully stocked pantries, a troop of workers, nannies, drivers and chefs, all at their beck and call, came to be considered normal.

Eight years later, after my three younger siblings came into this world, the scenario had become completely different from what I and my sister faced as they made the transition from poverty to wealth. The younger siblings were born into the comforts of plenty. They had a permanent nanny, access to exotic imported foods, gifts from abroad and designer clothes. My mother's compulsion to buy them things was so strong that I remember my older brother (still small) crying, asking not to be given any more presents. In reality, my three siblings grew up under a "contract with comfort", the bodily wellbeing and the right to live well, with a mentality that only seemed to know the extremes. My father Eusebio strove to protect them at all costs from a life of hardships, scarcity and unreasonable efforts, which is why he kept telling them that they did not need to work, that they could count on him and the fortune he had accumulated. This way of thinking led to various financial meltdowns, with serious consequences for everyone at home.

With regard to food, Rosa Isabel never liked cooking and paid for someone to take care of it at home (a common practice among affluent Colombian families).

She never had more than coffee and bread for dinner, just as she did at her mother Sofia's house. She adopted a rigorous midday ritual of repetitive intake of fruit, rice, fish and salad. I can't remember the last time I saw her eat anything else. In the process of finding out more about our food, I realised that it was unusual to have dinner at home. While lunch is the main

32

meal in many Colombian households and something lighter is served at the end of the day, there is always something for dinner. However, dinner was only prepared at home for my brothers (when they were small), and my father, Eusebio.

This dietary pattern eventually became entrenched. My mother, sister and I simply didn't eat dinner. There was no prohibition as such; *there was just no dinner* for women. While visiting my cousins' family, even though the family members only served something light for dinner, the women did eat. This was difficult for me and made me more anxious and hungrier. That's why I stuffed myself with sweets all day long, so I wouldn't break the no-dinner rule. I finally got used to saying that I didn't eat dinner. I even came to find it very strange that a woman would eat dinner at home.

As for my siblings, from their earliest years they began to show cracks in their relationship with food: my younger brother developed a certain apprehension towards food and a fear of mixing it because he claimed it was heavy for him, a problem that persisted into his forties; the other two spent their time experimenting with nutritional plans and a strong allegiance to the latest supplements on the market. Other disordered eating patterns emerged from adolescence, such as not eating for two to three days and then stuffing oneself to bursting. In general, food was a boring chore from which there was no escape.

For my part, although I did not develop anorexia or bulimia, I did have disordered eating and restrictive behaviours that posed high risks. I have lost count of just how many diets I tried in the first thirty years of my life. The way I saw it in those days, if I wasn't dieting, *I was gaining weight*, which was just so overwhelming. It was as if there was an ideal of a potentially achievable body, which always slipped through my fingers. The only way to get anywhere near that standard was to keep trying, and if I didn't, it was because of my many shortcomings. There was an assumption that the latest fad diet plan, the freshest, most innovative diet, would help me lose weight. Somehow, the idea was implanted in my mind that it was not ladylike to order steak and chips for lunch or dinner, because it was supposedly unladylike. This very same imagination dictated that ladies had glorious bodies and ate little, only allowing themselves salads, wholemeal carbohydrates and low-calorie drinks. I could thus sum up my experience in relation to food as influenced by a supposed normalisation of restrictive and disordered eating behaviours that posed an elevated risk to my health, because they were permeated by a culture obsessed with the body and low-calorie foods.

Many years later, while living in England, I fell victim to another food scam. This time it had to do with a pyramid scheme for selling products. Buying a nutritious protein powder with purported hunger-mitigating properties, I was convinced that it would change the entire bio-energetic structure of my organs and metabolism. It was as if some inner instinct compelled me to come up with a radical food solution of some kind, and so I bought up huge volumes of the product for my whole family.

It is difficult not to relate the multiple dietary restrictions and nutritional deficiencies to the resulting need to store, hoard and accumulate money in the lives of my father Eusebio and my mother Rosa Isabel. Based on the reaction of her children, it is possible that there was an eating disorder. My case was not so different. I too was overwhelmed in my search for solutions to major physical food problems. The absence of food at dinner triggered a desire in me to improve something. Years later, because I had access to my father's resources, I tried to "solve" my deficiencies immediately by investing heavily in diets and food supplements.

I unfortunately have more and more reasons to think that this kind of experiences of food restriction drawn from a family like mine are not so exceptional; indeed, I dare say that they are part of the same reality that seduces a high percentage of today's population, not only in Colombia where I was born and lived the first twenty years of my life, but also in England, my second home. When it occurs in so many socially and culturally different families, it is no wonder that the phenomenon is global.

There are also other types of eating disorders, such as **overeating** or **binge eating disorder**. I realised this when I first met the family of my husband Robert, a Briton of Italian and Irish descent (both true culinary kingdoms dominated by a devotion to foods rich in fats and sugars, sometimes in copious quantities). In his family, obedience or submission to the plate of food served was rewarded with affection, yet disdain was directed at the culture of restrictive, or "healthy" (vegetables and fruit) eating.

Robert jokingly reminisces about how the Italian and English families would get together for a meal on special occasions of the year. Everyone was looking forward to the Christmas meal, with its monumental menu. It began with an Italian *antipasto* starter consisting of choice pickles, hams and salad. This was followed by the main course (Neapolitan lasagne on one side, traditional English roast lamb with duck fat potatoes and braised vegetables on the other, all bathed in gravy). The crowning flourish came with the desserts: traditional "*English pudding*" (dried fruit tart flambéed in brandy with cream), followed by a cheese board, grapes, biscuits, wines and liqueurs. All this was served in a single meal.

Such eating occurred not only during the Christmas and Easter holidays, but also at weekends. When I met my mother-in-law Sarah, I witnessed her daily cycle of eating that went from restriction in the day to overeating at night. My mother-in-law, an English lady with an Italian name and countenance, restricted all food intake in the morning so that she could indulge herself in the afternoon with wines, biscuits, cheeses and chocolates. This was particularly prevalent after dinner and late into the night. Her kitchen and laundry room were more like a food storage centre, always overflowing with sweets, ice cream, biscuits and desserts.

During her childhood, London bore the brunt of the German bombing raids of World War II, while the country endured a period of forced food rationing. This experience may have triggered her anxiety issues and shaped her relationship with food. Her conversations always revolve about what she would eat (or what she should not have eaten). Sooner or later, she ended up talking about what she had been offered to eat, or what she wanted to buy in the supermarket. In the kitchen, she had her own personal drawer of favourite foods, which she guarded with suspicion.

Years ago, Sarah defied parental advice that she should marry a certain handsome Italian man. She picked an English boy: Billy, her boss at work, who had an Irish mother and a British father. Billy grew up in a family where all sorts of restrictions were in place. There were rules for everything.

Every belonging at home had to be counted, saved, cared for and reused. There was a prevailing contempt for wastefulness, something viewed as vulgar and akin to the "father of all vices". Billy's Irish mother, Niamh, had emigrated to London to take up a job as a domestic worker and there she met her husband, a policeman named Jacob. Niamh and Jacob had a strong set of rules at home, such as cleanliness, moderation, thrift and discipline. The eldest of three brothers (with two sisters), Billy's parents never had a house of their own, since they felt that saving money was preferable to squandering it on buying a house. They were terrified of debt and the very thought of a mortgage overwhelmed them. They spent their whole lives renting, despite having enough money to buy a house. The money they had saved in the bank and its value failed to sustain over time, so they lived in poverty, dependent on their children until their last days.

My father-in-law Billy disapproved of the way his father Jacob handled finances. He thought Jacob was too austere, stingy and rigid. Billy was open, spontaneous and sensible. He dreamt of the *good life*, and *good food*! He became interested in other things, such as the entertainment boom of the 1950s, shows and sports.

One of Billy's two sisters became obsessive about sports; the other developed a compulsive, undiagnosed dietary restriction. However, this second sister always lived with the fear of overdoing it, bursting at the seams, or just being *vulgar* because she craved food. She used to eat ridiculously small portions on exceedingly small plates. All this triggered a very severe digestive problem in her old age.

Billy, in the meantime, lived rather uninvolved in family life. When he met Sarah, the young assistant at his office, he found her different from other girls, not only because of her brilliance and proactivity, but also because of her Italian background and her exotic touch.

From another angle, my mother-in-law Sarah's experience of food responds, I believe, to the cultural patterns of her own family of origin. Her parents, Italian immigrants, had a discerning palate, an understanding of *good food*, and made their living in the restaurant business. As an only child, Sarah was thoroughly schooled in quality nutrition. Her family opened her up to the world of pizza, a "novelty" dish at the time, Italian ice cream, biscuits and assorted chocolates.

Sarah remembered a lonely childhood; she sat on the steps of the renowned restaurant looking out for the bustling Italian visitors and friends who came to see them, with no other company than themselves. There was always an atmosphere of abundance, parties and gatherings, even if at times it seemed a bit chaotic in interpersonal relationships, money management, and personal care. However, Sarah was educated in a Catholic convent school, where rules, restraint and emotional repression were the order of the day.

This odd pairing hinges on the attraction between Sarah (a woman who knows abundance in terms of cooking, financial ups and downs and comfort) and Billy (from a family steeped in limits, restrictions, rules and the "ought to be" of things). Unconsciously, my mother-in-law Sarah may have presumed that such a "system of rules" was much more appealing than the excesses at her parents' house. What is certain is that for Sarah and Billy, entertainment, good food, shows, and the places of luxury, became an essential element in their relationship as a couple: the glue that held the family together. This awareness of the social self, the version of themselves that exists in the eyes of the other, became what really mattered. As a result of applying it to feeding the household, Sarah endeavoured to cook up all sorts of tasty treats for the countless guests who always came to visit; her task was to *feed* and *entertain*. Of course, they didn't entertain just anyone, but respectable people with money, wealth or merit of some kind.

A close look at the elements of the family from one generation to the next reveals a system of binge eating or feasting combined with a certain rigidity in the psychic apparatus. Sarah's story is striking. Her mother, on the one hand, came from a wealthy and affluent Italian family from Amalfi—a privileged community—Strict, critical and somewhat severe, she married a modest Italian boy who was always on the edge of criminality, with shady dealings in London's black markets. He was friendly and charismatic, very sociable, even if his temperament hid his "explosive side". They married in haste, because of an unexpected pregnancy. They then went on to run a restaurant in London.

Sarah, the only child of these two offspring of immigrants, aspired to achieve her mother's social status, but in England. Because of her Italian roots, she always perceived herself as an outsider, *excluded* from the local people, all the more so in England where Italians were not well regarded during and after the war. Billy met Sarah's expectations of being closely linked to the local British group very well. After they married, Billy and Sarah lived in Sarah's parents' home for about three years. After working to raise enough money, they bought their own place. After eight years there, their sons Paul and Robert arrived.

My husband Robert's childhood experience in Sarah and Billy's home was one of loneliness. Robert recalls that his father was never home because of work. In fact, Billy came home to be looked after and to watch sports. He seemed self-absorbed. He usually spent weekends with his clients and friends playing golf, or bringing them to the theatre, a fancy dinner, or even home to entertain them. Robert never knew his father very well, since they did not have much in common. Sadly, he also spent no time with Sarah, who left him alone for hours at a time. Sarah herself even confessed to me repeatedly that she had always considered Robert a very difficult son, unlike his older brother Paul, whose behaviour, in her view, was impeccable.

My husband says that his mother fed him even when he wasn't hungry, not just to control his behaviour, but to spare herself the intake she craved. When Robert started gaining weight, she called him a "beached whale", saying he was clumsy, slow and useless.

It seemed that Sarah only knew how to give love through food, which is why it was important to eat whatever she put on the plate, even if you didn't want any more; otherwise, she perceived it as an affront and personal rejection.

Paul and Robert, Sarah and Billy's two sons, were an endless source of family entertainment, and deservedly so. Paul, the eldest, had a talent for music, played the piano incredibly well for his age and sang with virtuosity. In addition, he developed ice skating skills, had charisma, and was a good speaker, more like a charmer. He used all these talents to make his parents proud. Simply the idea of being able to casually mention in conversation a performance by Paul at a good theatre, or to show a trophy received for his

40

singing (casually displayed on the dining room table), became a recurring pleasure, a kind of ritual for the family. Life was all about impressing others.

Although Robert (my husband) had good grades in school, he received attention from his parents and family in a different way. His persistent tantrums and fits of anger at home and school gave his parents plenty of fodder for conversation and deliberation with neighbours, family and friends. His anger seemed to be easily appeased by sweets and tasty treats, or by just giving him whatever he most wanted. By his own account, there was no authority model, no cultural model or line of communication that set boundaries in the home, so he never knew how to contain and properly manage his emotional outbursts.

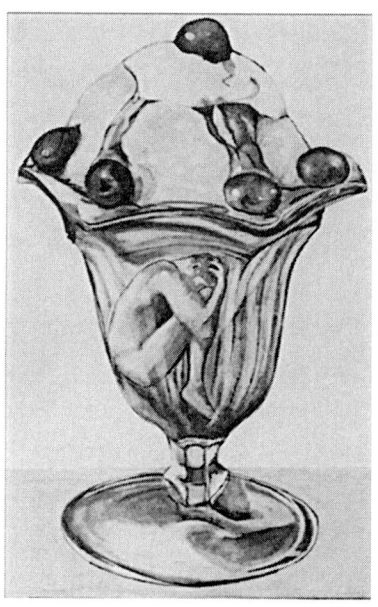

Drawing 2: *Emotional Hunger*, 2022

His accounts lead me to deduce that the family had a "mental hunger" that could not be satisfied by food alone. A need to experience moments of pleasure, to entertain the mind. That is why hobbies played an important role in the household. The television, for example, was always on, even when guests arrived, because it diluted conversations considered impertinent. Sports kept the family hooked on the scoreboards. Lottery tickets, horse races, musicals, card games, crosswords and puzzles all served to provide a constant stream of family fun, which meant that no one had to deal with personal, possibly painful, situations. Under the surface, there was a system of binge pleasure through entertainment and food, and emotional and affective restraint. There was also a complete absence of limits.

The genetic and environmental component emerging when examining the legacy of the two family backgrounds (Eusebio, Rosa Isabel, Sarah and Billy) may play a key role in explaining how their granddaughter developed this disease. For one thing, Eusebio and Rosa Isabel (my side of the family) had a domestic environment of food restriction and compulsive spending. Meanwhile Billy and Sarah (my husband Robert's family), lived in an environment of binge eating and emotional restraint in their home. Years later, it was Paul who developed a compulsive spending disorder, consisting of splurging money he didn't have, and food restriction. Paul was a smoker and a drinker.

However, this scenario does not necessarily guarantee the development of the disease, but I am convinced that the likelihood of developing ED in an environment such as the one I describe increases. If we now delve deeper into how the two families relate to the body, we can gain valuable additional information.

A history of attitudes towards the body

When I first began working with my therapist, I travelled down this avenue of family history at breakneck speed and tangentially, preferring to avoid it at all costs. In reality, I have never known anything but an atmosphere of criticism in relation to the body; there was something blurred, nebulous, about our experience of the body, and of the face: an obsession with bodily and facial beauty, and an infatuation with the idea of thinness.

I remember that conversations with my mother always revolved around physical appearance. She looked down on anyone who wasn't elegant, beautiful, slim, or who didn't have their hair styled by a hairdresser. In fact, she poured her scorn on poverty, as it annoyed her to see low-income earners. She showed her affection by helping her children to look smart, well-dressed and to associate with people who, in her opinion, enjoyed a good name and recognition. Whatever money my father earned from his work, she invested in personal care, for herself and everyone else at home. Facial beauty and body symmetry were central to her, and a good description of her own physiognomy.

Rosa Isabel, my mother, blonde and with very light blue eyes, was something really exotic and unusual in Colombia. Her Scandinavian heritage gave her an unusual and extraordinary foreign touch in the village where she lived for the first twenty years of her life. Her modelling gig at the local beauty parlour apparently nurtured in her the idea of dividing the world into beautiful and non-beautiful people, silently filtering our minds and family life with these prejudices. Sadly, only people with blue eyes and light hair, like my mother and my grandmother Sofia, were *beautiful*. I must point out that this way of seeing the world first reflects the state of cultural disruption in Colombia, where everything foreign outweighs anything local. The indigenous are undervalued and despised at every level and in every place, including their physical features.

This situation only became more acute in my family when my parents, Eusebio and Rosa Isabel, got together. Family members with indigenous features like Eusebio did not qualify as "beautiful". The matter created great difficulties, as only my older sister was considered to be "beautiful". My older brother with indigenous features (dark eyes and hair, genetically the same as my father) was taught as a child by his mother to say, with a certain mischievousness and liveliness, that he had blond hair, and that the true colour of his eyes, although it was not easy to see, was blue. Gradually the boy resolved to deny his physical qualities and claim he had blue eyes and blond hair, at least until he was five years old, which made everyone at home laugh. In this way, apparently harmless but not at all subtle, a tapestry began to be woven with shades of criticism, denial and condemnation of people with physiognomic characteristics typical of the Colombian environment, such as dark skin and black or brown eyes. Not to mention the "problem" of being fat (for women) and thin (for men), a stigma socially reinforced in my home through the typical system of nicknames designed to hurt and ridicule physical appearance.

Analysing the relationship of my family members with their bodies, I find that my three brothers (although never diagnosed with eating disorders or body dysmorphia) showed a great fondness for building muscle, eating high amounts of protein and spending long days in the gym, which, together with the rampant buying of beauty aids and treatments to rejuvenate, slim or widen the body, could well be considered a true *cult of the body*. Two of my brothers married women with body dysmorphic disorder (a mental illness characterised by an obsessive preoccupation with a minor defect or one that cannot even be perceived by others). One of them has suffered from bulimia from her youth to the present day, undergoing many surgical procedures to sculpt her body. Similarly, my other sister-in-law, driven by an obsession with her appearance, underwent multiple treatments, surgeries, diets and strenuous sports routines in order to achieve measurements that would give her a slim figure.

Simply put, our bodies have been a magnetic field that attracted the attention of everyone at home; that's why the investment of resources in beauty has been a constant for so long. Basically, what is restricted in food overflows into the body, through "self-care" and "body beauty", including anti-ageing efforts.

It is as if we are all determined to correct something, to improve or balance a loss. My brothers went about it by not only hoarding, stuffing and storing artificial food in their bodies (which somehow hid another deficit or more), but also by finding wives with similar deficiencies; the perfect match for them was a partner with a restrictive hobby or obsession.

In conclusion, the unresolved deficiency in the generations of yesteryear was inherited by the younger generation as a personal challenge, translated into an indiscriminate and unconscious search for the restitution of a fantasy balance that is out of control, due to the overflow of the precariousness that preceded us.

The perennial problem of a bulging belly

My earliest experience of difficulties with my body came a few days after I was born, in Duitama, where I am from, when my mother Rosa Isabel and my grandmother Sofía decided that my abdomen was too bulky and needed correction. My grandmother's paediatric student friend started prescribing medicines, potions and remedies to reduce the size of my belly. Seeing that their multiple home remedies did not work to bring down the growing bloating, they decided to admit me for emergency bowel surgery at the local hospital. Upon his arrival from training abroad, my father Eusebio was terrified of what was about to be done to his youngest daughter, a baby barely a month old. Taking matters into his own hands, he refused permission for the surgery and took me to a hospital in Bogotá, the country's capital. I was then discharged from the Military Hospital after they examined my badly infected gastrointestinal tract. They arranged for an emergency baptism so that I would not miss the Catholic rite of anointing of the sick, returning me to my family so that I could die at home.

I am told that Eusebio's relatives in Bogotá, Boyacenses with subsistence farming ancestors, took me into their care and began to give me teapots of broth made from cooking different vegetables mixed with baby formula. At that time, my aunt-in-law carried me in her arms all day long. After six months at my aunt and uncle's house, I became a case study who defied the odds at the Military Hospital in Bogotá.

As I grew up, I remember how my mother was troubled by my abdomen. *Always*. The fact that I was alive became an anecdote. She complained about my posture: that I should "tuck in my belly" or contract my abdomen, otherwise I wouldn't look slim, feminine or elegant. She knew all kinds of "remedies"; from the well-known "*stand up straight*" so that the "spilling" of the torso would not become evident, to the famous "belly-busting" pills, which produced severe diarrhoea. Nothing seemed to work. This led to all sorts of nicknames concerning my physical appearance. One frequent one was "*gorda popocha*", which in local slang refers to a person who is full, about to burst.

The way to express love, in my mother's case, consisted of trying to improve, correct, perfect, not only my appearance, but that of all the children, her husband, her siblings, her mother, in short, it was a never-ending job.

From the age of thirteen, my sister and I began to be taken to fashionable hairdressers, make-up classes, glamour, gymnastics, slimming massage sessions, cold wraps, facials, and all kinds of expensive beautifying treatments available in Bogotá. Incidentally, I remember with disappointment the visits to the diet centres, where the purpose was to talk to me about my fatness, to see if I would "become aware".

Looking back at my photos from this period, I see only a young woman burdened with her physical appearance, with nothing abnormal or physically repulsive, but who felt deformed.

Years later, when I was already married and living in England, I visited Bogotá. In a generous gesture, Mother scheduled a medical appointment for me at a local clinic. Mums are sometimes more concerned about their children's health than their own, so I was grateful when she urged me to take advantage of this "check-up". She used to go about her business in a secretive manner and without much explanation. I even thought I might be ill with something I hadn't realised, and in that case the best thing to do was to attend and clear up any doubts. When I arrived at the clinic, I discovered that it was a body aesthetics centre, and that the appointment was with a plastic surgeon, for pre-operative plastic surgery for a tummy tuck. I spoke to the surgeon and explained that it had all been a misunderstanding, as I had no intention of proceeding with the surgery.

Yo-yo dieting: gaining and losing weight

With regard to my husband Robert's family, it goes without saying that he always had in his mother (Sarah) a severe critic of the body. Her perfectionist tendency led her to see asymmetries and imperfections in every anatomy she observed. Everyone who came to my mother-in-law's house had to pass through her rigorous scrutiny, which included cold, incisive comments on the personal appearance, weight and clothing of guests and visitors.

Her stiffness and lack of compassion only reflected how she felt about her own body. For some reason, women of her generation (born in the 1930s), and generally those who had attended Catholic nunnery schools in London or were educated in convents or by religious orders of the same ilk, seemed to share a peculiar perception of the female body. A vision with difficulties in accepting the female corporeal reality in all its dimensions; sexuality, the natural functioning of our body, menstruation, in addition to the psychic and emotional component that identifies and exalts women, which allows them to lead, to be passionate, added to our capacity to be *spiritual*. However, Sarah made denigrating, disgusting and repulsive remarks towards women. The mere presence of another woman was perceived as a threat, as if by her judgements she wanted to correct an infraction in her own life.

Sarah felt guilty about her binge eating and her bulging body. She attempted to justify herself by recounting her countless visits and payments to the local Weightwatchers programme, where they assured participants that they could help them. All she did was to meet weekly with a group of people who followed the same dietary regime. They brought their scales and then weighed themselves one at a time *in public* (anyone present were referred to as witnesses and applauded the ones who managed to lose weight, even if it was just a few grams of fat). It was as if this slimming centre—which still exists—was using public shaming to force dietary restrictions, all in order to be able to report a certain weight loss in a defined time frame. I don't know if that centre succeeded in helping Sarah lose the weight she wanted so badly to get rid of; but I think it did create her habit of gaining and losing weight like a yo-yo, and becoming more and more "fat-phobic".

I was always aware of the complexity of her internal struggles. She struggled with a depressive, obsessive and controlling character. There is no way to describe her suffering after losing her husband, Billy, to cancer of the tongue, which later spread to the brain, and then her eldest son, Paul, in a mysterious car accident (yes, that beloved son who had been the light of her eyes). No wonder Sarah never had nice words to say about her own body, or Robert's body. My mother-in-law's difficulties in communicating contributed to the fact that her relationship with my husband was always marred by a low self-concept and constant condemnation of a part of her physical appearance that did not conform to her expectations.

In trying to understand how our experiences of the body in Colombia and England are linked to the development of ED in my daughter, a deficit of *physical acceptance* of the other becomes increasingly evident, both in my family and in my husband's family.

How to survive rejection at home: Body denial

Regardless of how my family or my husband's family approached the question of a proper relationship with the body, there is the way my daughter understood it and absorbed it from her own parents. Interwoven here is the difficulty Robert faced in excelling as a father and husband due to the myriad failings of support and affection in his family of origin, and my own limitations in accepting the female body as it is, seeking to get by with whatever resources were at hand.

My crusades in the midst of this environment veered towards a denial of my body; the very denial of my physical being, which throughout my life has cemented an open sanction of repudiation, attached to a tacit declaration of ugliness. This led me to a personal abandonment, to being in-visible, in-existent, in-valid; undeserving, failed and undesirable. Consciously or unconsciously, the indifference towards my body was read by my daughter as the very annihilation of a subject in its physical dimension. In exchange for giving up that battle, I opted for academic and intellectual development. I resolved to live life exclusively from my head. That is, affective restriction directed towards the body led to an academic binge or intellectual overfeeding of the brain.

Drawing 3: *Brain Hunger*, 2021

As I finished high school at the age of fifteen, I needed my father Eusebio's permission, in addition to child support, to go to university. He didn't see the point of my studying. He would often say: "What for? All you need to do is to work hard!"

I begged him to let me study, but he only agreed if he could choose the major. I thus enrolled in a university in Bogotá to study Business Administration, even though it was not my choice. Once I graduated, I begged him to let me fly to England to continue my studies. In London I found the support I never had in Colombia, and I managed to migrate towards research and social sciences. I completed two master's degrees (Human Resources and Political Theory) and a PhD at the London School of Economics and Political Science. There I worked as a research assistant and lecturer in the Sociology department. I continued my academic pursuits for a long time until I discovered art, a precious toolbox for growth where, without rules or pretensions, my head, the constant reasoning, finally found the place where *body and spirit* could be finally integrated.

My husband, on the other hand, chose to put his body to use and devoted himself to the performing arts and entertainment. His life project focused on Italian operas, while training as a tenor. I found the lyrical singing of his voice to be a dramatic and guilty call from within him, seeking his mother's acceptance. With regard to food, a pattern developed of using food as a means of emotional release. Any unresolved difficulty, rejection, neglect or seemingly out of control situation triggered him to explode, and his ideal solution was food, entertainment, sports or operatic music. Years later, Robert managed to leave singing behind, realising that his body never really met all the physical requirements for it, founded his own market research company and proved that it was possible to change his career successfully.

Robert's life thus came to include two intergenerational pendulum systems. From binge eating to the restriction of compassionate acts and affection on the one hand and from compulsive comfort and entertainment to the restriction of empowerment on the other (generating in turn feelings of victimhood and guilt).

By establishing himself as a director of his own company, my hope is that Robert will begin to take control of his relationship with the world around him, care of his body and mind, his emotions and affections.

By managing to recognise the lines that situate us in reality, give us perspective and suggest the horizon, I was able to draw the need to get out of this sketch of intergenerational illness. It now seems inconceivable to me that at one time I myself helped to maintain an illusion of physical and mental health within our families.

Noticeable patterns in both families

A closer examination of the two families reveals a common denominator beyond the pendulum swing from bingeing to restriction and vice versa. The first element that strikes me is the encounter between food and guilt.

An Atmosphere of Guilt

There is a common pattern shared by the two families of origin (Rosa Isabel and Eusebio; Sarah and Billy) and it is a feeling of guilt in the family atmosphere. Such guilt may well have permeated all areas of our lives including our relationship with the body and food throughout the generations.

On my family's side, I argue that the guilt stemmed in part from my father Eusebio's impoverished past. I remember my conversations with him, and his stories embellished with humour. However, as a child growing up in a village far from the capital, Eusebio had to face the lack of the minimum basic resources necessary for a dignified existence as a human being. He remembered running through the paths of a rural town in Boyacá at the age of six, dressed only in shorts and no shoes. Years later the local parish priest chose him for the path to become a Catholic priest. Part of his training involved visiting low-income families. That was when he vowed never to return to such work again. In his own words, Eusebio explained that he could see no solution to local poverty through a church lacking resources, and deduced that such relief could only come from the generation of resources *by hand*. Thus, through hard work and dedication, Eusebio got a job in a local wing of the Ministry of Agriculture, which later sent him to train in Israel. On his return, he found employment helping destitute farming communities. His contacts with the Dutch merchant fleet enabled him to become the exclusive distributor of agricultural commodities in the country.

The abundance of his pantry aroused his guilt: at himself, at his forgotten people, at his neglected living ancestors who continued to experience physical and emotional hunger, or perhaps at his parents who died as a result of the famines; I don't know. Surely the guilt of a full cupboard was no match for the panic of an empty one. Eating with him was awkward. He developed a series of rituals that began by ensuring that, before eating, he had personally fed beggars, the elderly or anyone around him who was vulnerable or helpless. Our house always had guests, people we mostly didn't know. Once he brought a beggar and called us to attend to him, give him food and serve him.

This guilt component has had a big impact on my life. I see it in my attitude when I think that I must work without rest, move without stopping, serve the needy, always think of the other and forget about my own needs. Hence, I find it difficult to enjoy food without having done something to "earn that food", with the negative repercussions this has had on my daughter.

Undoubtedly, my father's alcoholism is another component. All of us who are children of an alcoholic parent know the family atmosphere surrounding the alcoholic and the guilt it generates.

On my husband's side, Sarah, his mother, felt a great deal of guilt and shame associated with her eating. As a child, her parents, Italian immigrants, were in the restaurant business in London. They worked all day and didn't spend much time with her, so she felt she was a burden, a heavy burden on them. In reality, Sarah grew up alone, without affection or boundaries. She was twelve years old during the food rationing of the Second World War and had the luxury of access (without any restrictions) to a wide range of foodstuffs, which was completely unheard of at the time. All because her parents were licensed meal providers. Today I understand that, far from making her feel lucky and grateful, Sarah's parents contributed to her accumulated food cravings, coupled with her shame that drove her to eat for reasons not necessarily related to physical hunger.

In addition, her father Vittorio suddenly and without explanation disappeared during the war. It was years before she learned that Vittorio had been hiding in the same neighbourhood where she lived, just to save himself the trouble of compulsory military service. Learning of this filled her with anger, shame and contempt for the actions of her parents and family, as it turned out that they had all colluded to keep the secret. Once married to Billy, Sarah changed her Italian first name to English and adopted her husband's British surname. As if that wasn't enough, she dropped her accent and went to live in an affluent English neighbourhood.

It was not until the day of her funeral that many of her old friends learned not only of her real first name, Simonetta Marino, but also of her Italian ancestry in Naples and Amalfi; What's more, none of them knew the details of her background in the impoverished streets of Tottenham, in the heart of London, as the daughter of Italian immigrants. This brings us to another common element in both families, pretending to be what we are not.

Boasting: Another Common Denominator

Definitely another element present in our family that has required work is the uprooting of pretentious attitudes. Undoubtedly, the habit of boasting about being *what we are not*, of believing ourselves to be more than the people around us, can manifest itself in various ways in today's world. One of these is *avoidance*, a psychology term used to describe the behaviour of some people who tend to procrastinate, to disengage from work or an obligation and put it off. Avoidance involves not facing situations and not taking responsibility; blaming the other person, and even creating white lies and fantasies in the mind to justify this attitude.

The way Sarah pretended to be someone she was not had a great impact on my husband Robert and his brother Paul, for whom the fantasy of comfort, wanting to be "special" at all costs and gravitating towards the exclusive spaces of lineage and pedigree were a real priority. Procrastination has always been easier than coping and solving. And in saying so, I withdraw any value judgement. Avoidance simply sticks to comfort at times and attaches importance to it. It is a strong self-protection mechanism.

Interestingly, Rosa Isabel seemed to be very in tune with Sarah in this respect, even though they had never met, since one was in England and the other in Colombia. However, the idea of starting something, escaping from a broken home, and making a fresh start in a seemingly better place were legitimate and understandable desires in both cases. The difficulty arises in trying to ignore and even erase who one really is, and to start moulding a completely different person, pretending that she has always lived in that new community. What this attitude implicitly achieves is to condemn one's own roots, ethnicity, history and biography, with serious psychological consequences. Dissociations are created, internal conflicts, the need to hide, to secretly enjoy "the known" and to put up with problems and situations of others, just to remain in a fictitious and lonely place. The fear of "being discovered" begins to overwhelm the mind, generating paranoia and acute contradictions that are difficult to assimilate and resolve naturally.

Pretentious living, on the other hand, is capable of creating tools that "cushion" the suffering of the past; we could compare pretentiousness (whatever its size) to a childish way of coping with life. Eusebio, my father, might have made more of his fortune if this pretentious attitude had knocked on his door. He never got that close. Apparently, the easiest way to assimilate the *pretentious life* is through *osmosis*, transfer by contact; a minimum dose of will and reflection is enough to achieve this. When socialising with others with the same condition, certain mannerisms, habits and beliefs begin to be acquired, to the point of self-belief. The family provides a perfect setting for this. Rosa Isabel did not manage to pass on enough of this attitude to her husband, but she did to her eldest daughter. Perhaps the fact that Eusebio spent much more time in peasant communities than at home vaccinated him against the flourishing "pretence syndrome" at home. Undoubtedly, a pretentious environment often carries a serious risk: neglect or stubbornness in the face of the reality that needs attention.

In my experience, a pretentious environment is based on premises such as: "*Bad things don't happen to me because I'm good, I pay taxes, I come from a good family, I eat vegetables, I'm religious...,*" etc. In short, even if the idea is not verbalised but tacitly assumed: "*I am not like the people to whom bad things do happen, I am above them*", by thinking and feeling this way, we are deliberately closing our eyes, for example, to the reality of a complex medical diagnosis. This was precisely the "Achilles' heel" in the case of Sarah and her family, as she failed to recognise the mental health difficulty that afflicted Paul, her eldest son. Paul's chronic lying warranted a psychiatric evaluation. He would develop *impostor syndrome* years later, a pathology consisting of a fear of being considered "boring" (or an ordinary person), and to avoid this, the sufferer lies through his teeth. Sadly, Paul went on to become a criminal, perpetrating frauds that allowed him to bluff and squander money on sports cars and luxurious mansions, all at the expense of the fraud victims in his path. Such a distressing situation quite possibly generated an atmosphere of guilt in the whole family.

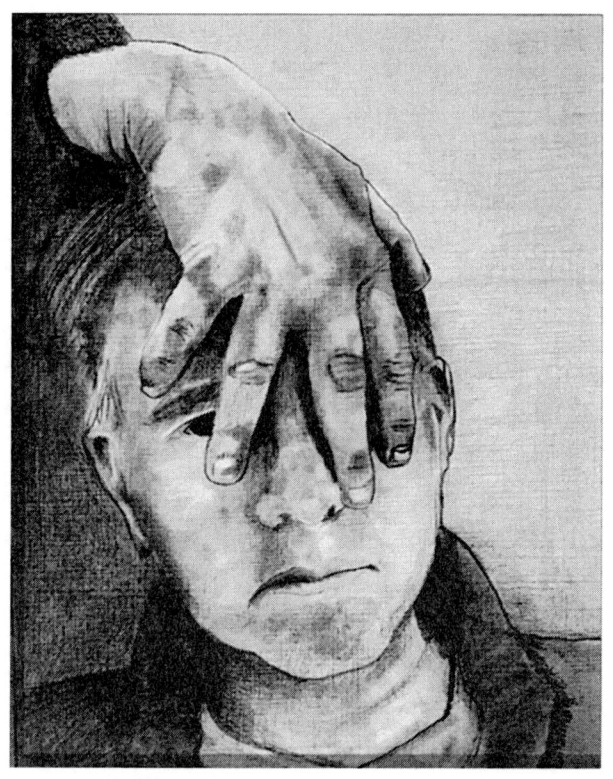

Drawing 4: *I Pretend I Did Not See*, 2022

My husband and I were also contaminated with pretentious feigning, in one way or another. Even when we seemed aware of the reality of the presumption in our respective mothers, we proved perversely adept (or just a couple of experts, if you will) at silencing the internal alarms. An internal psychic alarm is triggered when something important requires our attention. Robert and I "turned off" the alarms simply because *we knew how to do it*. When my daughter got sick, Robert didn't want to see it. As for me, I saw it but dismissed it as a passing thing. It was my way of not appearing troublesome, difficult or burdensome in the eyes of the other. This is how the opinion of the other displaces what should really be considered "*of supreme importance*".

I believe that the inner sensitivity, the instincts, the unconscious that comes with each of us, that activates the spiritual life and awakens the sense of transcendence, is also concerned with orienting the social being to what others think, and can be vital not only in our interpersonal relationships but in defending life itself. If that sensitivity is dormant, neutralised, or silenced by the stridency of other voices and overflowing desires, it will eventually go unnoticed, leaving the self-care and mental health of ourselves, our children and grandchildren adrift.

Therapeutic exercise in our family posed a daunting challenge. We chose to push through the burden of the past and commit to understand our reality; advocating for transparency to be the family we are, as human beings, individuals, a couple and as parents: completely fallible and limited in our resources to help our daughter. We have learned from hard experience that *pretentious arrogance* is counterproductive. Simply because it creates an atmosphere of falsehood, secrecy and mistrust for everyone at home.

And how did we break this *pretentious* and *false confidence*? Allowing the feeling as it comes, and the being, to be, letting it express itself freely, putting the easy and the difficult on the table to listen to it. Opening ourselves to that inner sensitivity that allows us to be and act physically, emotionally, creatively and spiritually. Taking responsibility for the actions and decisions we take, understanding that this builds the course of one's life. Stop blaming the other, closing our eyes to what is in front of us that deserves attention, compassion, listening and acceptance. Ultimately, we are talking about the permission we give ourselves *to be who we are*; a commitment to integrity in what we say, what we do and how we feel about it. Our determination at home to abandon the pretence of a life that is not our own has led us to walk a new path: **walking in accordance with who we are**. This decision reawakens the lost inner sensitivity, allows each of us to hear the echo of that voice again, and outwardly, the very essence of being is evident and manifests itself in all our actions, no matter how cumbersome, abnormal, irregular, or irrational they may seem to others. When we erase our self-judgement, we open the door to freedom.

We have been discovering together that the reservations of a stealthy, secretive and hermetic life among family members are harmful, especially when dealing with a disease such as ED, whose high component of "hidden" decisions generates so much guilt.

History of Mental Health Disorders

Genetics has also played an important role in the development of the disease in our family. After identifying the history of family members affected in their mental health, it is not surprising that the same illness is present among the young people of this generation and those who barely "seek for some orientation". I must confess that mental health issues have arisen in a variety of ways in both Robert's family and my own, as clinical depression, schizophrenia, successful suicides, anxiety, alcoholism and smoking, not to mention undiagnosed illnesses such as EDs. Although certain mental illnesses are more common than others in families, it cannot be said that if one family member has symptoms, then everyone will develop them, but it does increase the risk. There are undoubtedly many other risk factors and the issue goes beyond what I can cover in these lines, but let us say that, in general terms, our two families of origin presented, in addition to the above, extreme fears or worries, anxiety and strong guilt.

While these mental disorders are treatable today, none of these family members received medical treatment or primary care, so they all deteriorated with age. For example, in her seventies, my mother-in-law Sarah lived in a constant state of anxiety, and refused to receive the treatment medication that could help her because she feared the side effects. Sadly, towards the end of her days she became extremely aggressive. My father Eusebio lived pretending that his large alcohol intake could be compatible with his very limited food intake. Although his mind was in perfect condition, his body could not withstand the abuse he endured over his final years. Paul, my husband Robert's brother, became depressive and ran into anxiety problems after committing major scams on many people, including his own family, dying in Thailand in mysterious conditions. When mental illness occurs, I believe it is important to affirm a commitment to the truth, to the health of those dealing with it directly. Otherwise, how will their quality of life improve?

In conclusion, while I can hardly argue that my daughter was immune to factors transmitted from her family environment that may have contributed to the development of the disease, these factors do not, by themselves, determine its onset. As we shall see later, there are other important elements in the context of the patient's life from conception, her personal traits and characteristics (including her own personality and character, together with traumatic experiences).

The good news is that, as much as we must take these and any other risk factors into account, they are neither an ironclad condemnation nor the end of the road.

III
Individual Characteristics: Childhood and Personality

Pregnancy

My daughter's birth and childhood were important periods in her case study. During the first twelve weeks of pregnancy, I was at risk of miscarriage on several occasions, and at one point the doctors at Middlesex Hospital in England opted for a CVS (chorionic villus sampling), which is used to examine the baby and explore possible genetic problems. I was warned that the result was very possibly positive for Down's Syndrome.

That statement unleashed a storm inside me. The hospital started making calls to schedule a termination and suggested a "clean slate".

The outlook was unclear to me. My health was not good, I was not gaining weight and I preferred to wait until I felt better. Frightened and in a sea of doubt, with daily nightmares from the hospital's constant calls to reconsider "a new beginning", I decided to keep waiting. I was referred to preventive obstetric care, as my urine protein levels warranted a renal work-up. In the fourth month of pregnancy, I made the decision to move forward, join groups of parents of babies with Down's Syndrome, devour related literature and prepare for the arrival of my child. In the seventh month, after the amniocentesis test, they called me to "confirm" that the baby *did not have Down's Syndrome.*

Maybe it was the shock of information and expectations, or maybe it was meant to be; the fact is that my baby was born premature. Good size for her age, although very slim. When she was born, she only wanted to be with me, breastfeeding. The little hands, always very tightly clasped, gave me the impression that she was a nervous baby.

During her first year of life, she was very sensitive; to cold, heat, noise and being left alone. Her stomach could not tolerate formula milk. Her intolerance extended to certain foods by the time she was two years old. The first time she tried the ice cream her legs swelled so much that we had to take her to the doctor. The cheese caused a very visible and painful stomach distention. Persistent bowel movement difficulties turned into visits to the specialist. At the age of three, the doctor suggested removing all preservatives from her diet. This food restriction, while effective in that it resolved the allergic reaction, was not without its problems, as this was the age when children try a lot of sweets, ice cream and colourings in many foods. Her teachers were sad to see her always eating healthy food when the other children were tasting all kinds of sweets. It was certainly difficult for my daughter, although she did her best (sometimes in an exaggerated, desperate and even obsessive way, I admit), wanting to be a good girl. Already at that time, a certain perfectionist touch flashed in her, present in her high sensitivity to noise, to the textures of clothes, and in the insinuation of artistic traces in her personality at all levels.

Once the food restriction imposed by the doctor was lifted, my daughter became very hungry, or ate for the taste of her freedom. She was feeding ceaselessly, with some anxiety. My husband is a very tall man, and so is she, so I didn't mind too much when they went overdid it. Moreover, my own experience of not being able to eat at dinner time compelled me to let her eat when she needed to.

Only when my husband alerted me that her intakes were already excessive for her ten years, did I hesitate to let her eat what she was asking for. I noticed that my daughter was eating at high speed, like her father. Comments about being overweight began to follow us wherever we went. Grandmothers, in particular, did a lot of damage with their laughing remarks laden with poison for the soul of a sensitive, intelligent child, who urgently needed to be surrounded and accepted unconditionally. Thus, after a short phase of overfeeding, the restrictive phase began through dieting and at the age of eleven: purging and fasting. The girl, who had gained height in a relatively short time, grew three centimetres in height in six months, while losing 16 kilos.

At this point, my daughter was expressing a reality that was present in the entire family. With her own personality, courageous and silent, her life itself shouted the urgency of our intergenerational and transatlantic illness; the vitiated way we relate to ourselves, to the body and to food. She was just another vulnerable member of the family, highlighting a problem deeply rooted in our ancestors from long ago.

I didn't want an ED, I wanted to lose weight

My conversations with my daughter about how ED started helped me to understand that ED comes not only where it is welcomed, but that its presence is *harmless, familiar and friendly*.

If it were a person and not just an impersonal antagonistic force (which makes a lot of sense to those of us who have had to delve into the matter), I would describe it as a good-natured, strong and reliable mythical entity that has sensational ideas for bringing about longed-for change. She says that losing weight was a project that encouraged her, as everything was going wrong in her life, both the first phase (which she lived in Colombia) and the second (in England).

Drawing 5: *ED Arrived*, 2021

Regarding my daughter's experience with the family I come from, although she was born in England, we lived in Colombia for three years (her pre-school years); otherwise, we visited them regularly during her childhood and youth. Sadly, life in Colombia was not easy for her; her light blonde hair eventually turned deep brown and she used to grumble about not having blue eyes. I did not know at what point all this information of what was "acceptable" and "beautiful" in my family of origin in relation to the face and body was transferred with high effectiveness. The point is that she experienced it as painful and very real.

Her classmates at her public school in England, where she was a scholarship holder, looked down on her in the canteen, because of the way she ate and her size. Whenever she sat down, the others would leave the table. So when they suggested a diet, she wanted to invest all her energy in achieving it. According to my daughter, the popular girls knew all about fad diets, and they looked fabulous: they were blonde, light-eyed like her Colombian grandmother (Rosa Isabel), and very thin. They belonged to the British upper class (as their other grandmother, Sarah, aspired to). In short, they were everything she was not, *and everything she had been wrongly taught she should be.*

Gradually, this *entity* that we have already identified as a dangerous illness (the ED), capable of perversely slimming us to death, becomes a guide with very clear rules on how to achieve its sinister goal. When dealing with an ED, it offers some certainty to its victim, and how necessary certainty has become for a young person in this world full of unanswered questions and cruel realities!

It is in this way that *losing weight* becomes a fantasy of a better life, a world where one is popular, beautiful, valued; where one can occupy a better place in the dreamed gallery of dignity and respect, be heard, be **free**. The price of all this: *being slim*. A well-known price, *familiar* to my daughter. She had heard it a thousand times at home and at her grandmothers', so there was nothing to be alarmed about. A diet was both *normal* and *necessary*. Restricting food was the way to go.

The beginning of this new phase under the tutelage of the seemingly friendly "protective entity", the ED, became an unfathomable labyrinth, an unpredictable journey. My daughter's steps through this life now had not only a *faithful friend* with "*certainties*" about what to do and what not to do, but a leader, who took charge of everything that frightened her. It numbed her and even completely invaded her mind with a new weight-loss project.

My daughter became "transformed" in this process and her identity was eclipsed: she wanted to be someone else. Surrendering her rights was a viable alternative for her. It was her chance to try a new road, as at the time she lacked the tools to cope with her painful experiences, because of the path that was opening up in front of her. Her brain software then began to run with abandon.

I think that the total submission to ED, the rules of the resulting subordinate relationship, already existed in my daughter's "software" before the onset of the disease. The disorder harnesses *already existing* software and moves through these corridors of obedience, servility perfected through obsession. The disease is therefore *relational*, a type of relationship in which the young woman loses her empowerment. The central part of the *psyche* that calls for order is missing, and disease, seeing the empty chair, sits on the throne to rule.

For someone to agree to align themselves with personal abandonment of this magnitude, they must have experienced a priori abandonment at home and at school. Similarly, the boy or girl had to experience unmet needs from parents, grandparents, teachers or caregivers, offensive messages questioning their worth (implicit or direct), or the invalidation of their emotions of pain, cold, hunger, fear, loneliness, uncertainty or anger. Most likely there were also demands to ignore being a child or young person and assume adult roles, inappropriate for their age.

Frighteningly, physical symptoms such as prolonged hunger, stomach pain, heartburn (from an empty stomach) and headaches almost take a back seat to the *fear of disobeying* the totalitarian regime imposed by the ED. It is for this reason that, although EDs are experienced through food, it is not really always about fear of the food itself (although this is often the case), but fear of *the consequences of tasting the forbidden food*, fear of fatness, of being heavy, of taking up large spaces, of taking on the present, of facing it as it comes and *making a presence*. It is fear of living the life you have and where you have it. Fear of feeling too much, fear of getting angry and upset, of breaking the rules of the game, of questioning and finding that not all people who claim positions of authority are of equal value. Unfortunately, emotion management and ED are intricately linked. This is why personal and physical stagnation is due to a need to *protect oneself* from a "threatening" external environment, in which it is supposedly no longer viable to grow.

What appears to be a young woman dieting is in reality a renunciation, a contract of allegiance in exchange for the certainty of an "achievement". This contract with the manipulating entity gains strength as host and guest lose each other; the ED, now as host, feeds on obedience. By gaining voice and impact in her mind, the ED reminds her not to eat certain fattening foods. In the words of my daughter: "it's like a good friend who gradually starts to take food away from you". Sadly, far from being a friend, it is a self-proclaimed dictator, infamous and deceitful. What begins as a suggestion becomes an imposition, a high-ranking order that cannot be reversed. It is a 24-hour-a-day life of accountability to a ruthless and hostile tyrant. Carbohydrates, fats and abundant food seem equally abhorrent, untouchable, destructive and toxic. If she ate some calorically dense food, she would go to the toilet to vomit it up.

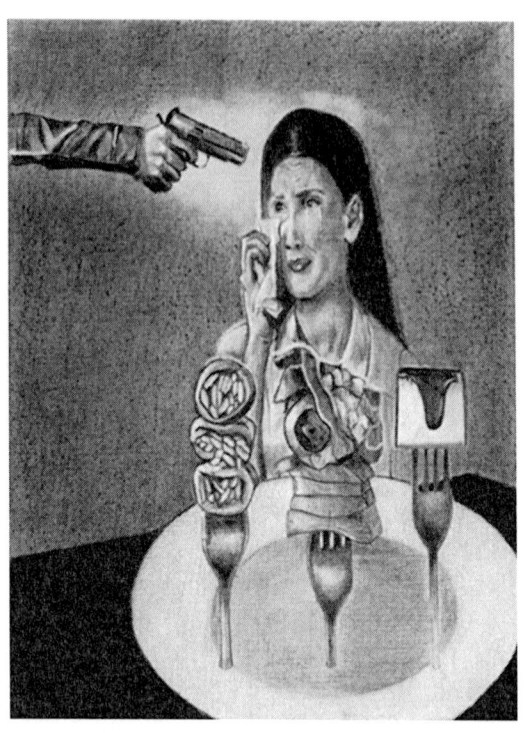

Drawing 6: *Fear Of Food*, 2022

The disease lures the youth into following a precise and complex route, full of obsessive, compulsive and depressing laws and dictates. My daughter's mind was simply filled with a cloud of to-dos dictated by the disorder, a lengthy list that included exercise, academic performance, non-stop calorie counting and not sleeping. Hunger even leads many patients to show symptoms of infantile regression. During the early stages of the disease, my daughter asked for baby compotes and cutlery, food in small buckets, and to be able to lie down in the foetal position. In a paralysing way for everyone at home, the illness itself convinces the afflicted child that there is no disease or need for medical attention because the child is not as sick as others who deserve immediate medical attention.

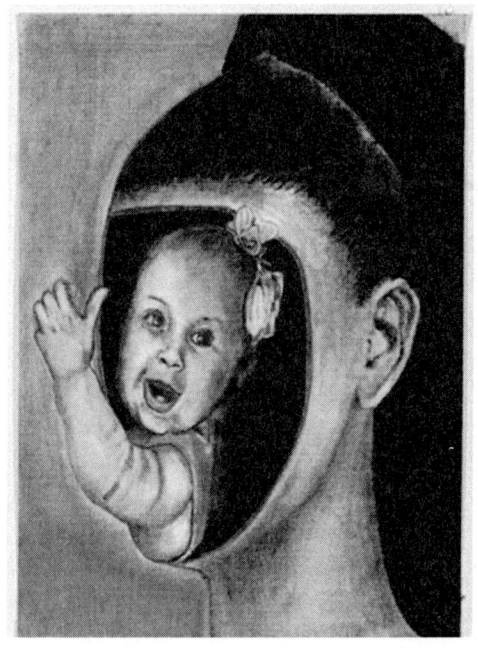

Drawing 7: *Regression*, 2022

The expected body changes began to recast with the disease (under such a tyrannical regime, it was no surprise that she found none of the promised certainties when she looked in the mirror). The psychosocial development, meanwhile, was blunted. All age-related processes, in her case, were pushed into a corner; the adolescent's task of settling into a new body that is growing and developing was altered, partially or totally. The phase of self-questioning, the awakening to the present, the past and the future, was cut short. Her fears, characteristic of her age, were magnified, such as the possibility of being left homeless. The images on the news (which terrify anyone) affected her even more; her anguish and distrust began to multiply day by day.

Drawing 8: *Fear Of Life, ED Is My Friend*, 2022

As if that wasn't enough, when my daughter started to lose weight, the whole world applauded. Starting *with me, my husband, and the grandmothers…* I admit to being relieved to find that my daughter was no longer eagerly eating the quantities she used to. I thought she had completed the stage of receiving additional food to sustain her fore coming body's growth. In reality, she began to disappear, and this hid the terrifying reality of her suffering.

By way of illustration, the bite of a baboon monkey rests not only on the power of its sharp fangs, but also on the high risk of contracting the rabies bacteria, which needs time to develop. Likewise, ED has a sharp and very deep sting, with the potential to affect a person's physical, mental and relational performance.

Drawing 9: *The Grip Of The Disease*, 2021

The therapeutic process should dismantle the foundations of this structure that is present and that establishes a hierarchical system responsible for intervening in all interpersonal relationships. The young woman, dwarfed in her self-esteem, has as a common denominator in every reading of life a constant tendency to minimise her value and importance. ED becomes a gradual annihilator of being. Only by dismantling the structure that blurs the young woman's worth, voice and vote, her autonomy and authority, will she be able to conceive the idea of rebelling, and do it successfully, against the executioner; a strategy to react and silence or at least minimize the voice of the ED with her own voice and authority. This requires a nurturing and courageous brain and body; my daughter needed and still needs validation, understanding, respect, love and boundaries.

In conclusion, my daughter suffered a challenge of major proportions at a very young age, through a stressor-weakened, sick and anxious mother. She was already carrying a latent vulnerability at birth: *born hungry*, i.e., there were deficiencies from birth, which possibly manifested themselves mentally in her behaviour of wanting much more, and on a physical level in her reaction of intolerance to food. By starting a restrictive plan at such an early age I can only infer that a pattern of avoidance was established with serious consequences for her future life.

There is a factor that reinforces and enhances the compendium of variables discussed so far in these brief lines, and that is the amount of messages that multiply in the media and communication platforms, in the hands of increasingly younger influencers who do not always care much about the scope of what they say or transmit, not to mention the work already done by television and magazines that (with some honourable exceptions) still promote stylised thinness, and the ideal of beauty based on body and facial symmetry.

IV

The Environment

A full recovery from an ED in this century requires a thorough awareness of the *toxic messages* that can delay a person's true freedom with false hopes and expectations. This call is not only for people who suffer from an ED or face it at home, but for all of us who are captive audience of advertising and marketing, of social media that through their algorithms fill us with dietary rubbish every minute, and expose us to develop the disease in our old age while enslaving today's new generations.

I was shocked to learn that every 52 minutes a person dies as a direct result of an eating disorder (STRIPED, 2020). This concerns us all, because we are all connected in one way or another, since one person's pain is *everyone's*. Moreover, the most wonderful news here is that one generation can reverse the pain of many.

Yet, in the age of freedom of expression (which, although it does not exist in many parts of the world), how is it possible that it is still taboo to confront food and body standards just to please the billion-dollar industry that supports fashions, diets and protein supplements to reduce fat and increase muscle?

The question that burst into my step-by-step climbing process to understand this issue in depth was: what is wrong with us as a society, that we are destroying ourselves with unhealthy eating patterns and absurd body standards? How is it that so many of us fall like flies and end up in the web of this subtle sophistry of distraction, dreaming of looking ever more sculpted, thinner, more fragile, only to end up more "invisible", erasing even the lines that define our identity?

For all of us who are passionate about freedom today, this motivates us to help identify this absurd reality of existential slavery. Knowing that we can contribute to changing lives fills us with purpose, and encourages us to question this quest for miracle food and phantom bodies.

As an active recipient of this message of aesthetics and thinness, I lived under the delusion that our conventional ideals of beauty (symmetrically chiselled bodies and faces) were admirable; like being dazzled by a flower, or the natural wonders of this planet. Unperturbed by its effects, I was a passive accomplice to the pain and illness of a population suffering from body dysmorphia (one cannot help but think of one or more perceived defects), bulimia, anorexia, or all of them together, as became the case with my daughter.

Living an entire life moving from one diet or dietary restriction to another, hoping for an otherworldly body, is to move in a fantasy scenario. Likewise, embracing the conviction that over-exercising in a gym or running as a means of compensation is laudable, only threatens life. Populations that constantly reduce and exaggerate their caloric intake, restrict an entire food group, or ceaselessly exercise in pursuit of a sculpted, "lean" or exaggeratedly muscular body exhibit what in ED medical circles are called *risk behaviours.* However, this has become "normal" nowadays.

We have been infamously conditioned to despise the flesh of the body, its weight, the fatty component, its presence and freshness. To "spare ourselves the trouble" we silenced the inner voice that alerts us to what is not right in our environment. For example, we are paying for products and services to look scrawny and symmetrically perfect in the certainty that this ideal brings happiness, without questioning what really drives this behaviour. We are also witnessing how the fashion industry promotes malnourished and vulnerable young people to wear very small clothing sizes on the catwalks, which unconscionably embarks them on an unsustainable level of physical emaciation. When we buy into a concept of skeletal beauty, we become complicit in a serious attack on today's children, who desperately seek out models, admire them and then replicate them.

The deception comes from the normalised judgement that says: "being fat is bad, because it means you are unhealthy, while being thin is good because it means you are healthy". It is possible to be obese and healthy and it is possible to be thin and sick. Both extreme thinness and excessive obesity merit psychological and possibly psychiatric care and attention, not because of the way an individual looks, but because of the impact on the person's quality of life, functionality and achievement of personal goals. The issue cries out for attention to the prevailing definitions of **what health actually means** in our times. The tendency to think of all fat people as slow, unproductive, overweight and vulgar needs *immediate reassessment* as it alerts us to how sick we are as a society. We have unconsciously held on to this assumption as true.

The implication of such a decision is that we end up promoting generations of young people who are perfectionists, anxious, obsessed with doing, with achievement, with malnourished bodies and without the right to rest and a much-needed break.

Drawing 10: *Is This What We Aspire To?* 2022

V

Why My Daughter?

At the end of this intergenerational journey and the associated factors that may have opened the door to ED in my daughter, I return to the initial question: *why did this happen to my daughter?* Looking at it from another, more informed perspective helps me understand that, while I've held on to this question for a long time, the simplest answer is: *Why not her?* However, there are contexts and environments that are conducive, latent genetics, internal and external factors that play a role, such as personality traits and social pressures. We are also confronted with age-old cultural beliefs about the body and food, and must learn to discern the times and destructive agents that allow a disease to germinate and colonise the mind and body of the victim, affecting their entire family, and new generations.

She had several of these factors, which facilitated the invasion of an ED.

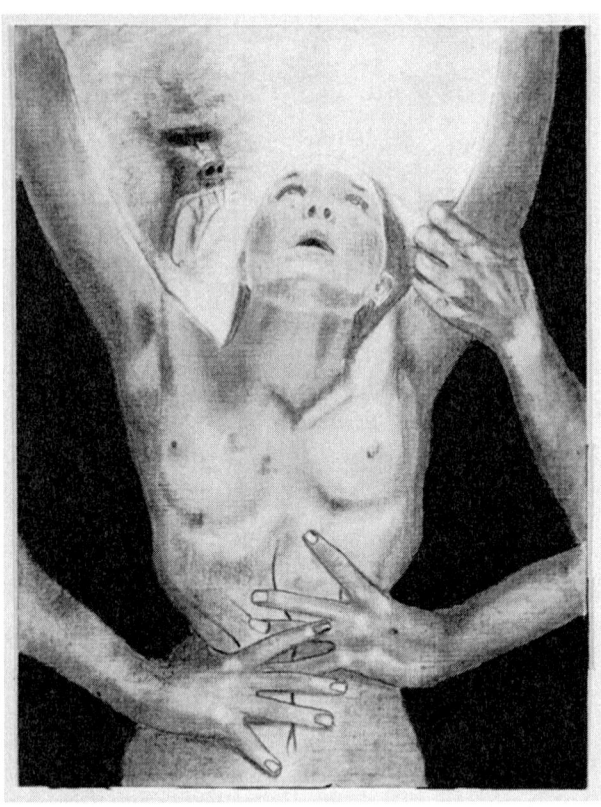

Drawing 11: *Help*, 2022

The intergenerational story of binge eating to restraint (the chapter on the nuclear family of her father and mother), the difficulties encountered during pregnancy, in addition to some of her personality traits such as her high intelligence, her creative, artistic, hypersensitive side, coupled with her anxiety, and her tendency to be a bit obsessive and perfectionist in managing her relationship with the world around her, may have catapulted her to the centre of the disease. She also lived through an accumulation of painful experiences, some unjust, some cruel, all in the midst of abandonment, without guidance or any clear boundaries; and most deplorable: *without the necessary tools to protect herself.* This traumatic experience has needed attention for many years. By not understanding what we were up against and how to deal with it at the appropriate time, an ED took root, becoming, ironically, a coping mechanism. It numbed her, disconnected her, and provided her with an alternative plan, a new path, a route that relieved her of the pain of the latent reality; this made it attractive, necessary, beneficial, and at times addictive.

Paradoxically, the ED, in a way, sustained my daughter. It was the best *known* way of coping with deep pain, while helping her stave off that inaccessible psychic discomfort. This collection of traumatic events she went through in her childhood and youth can be compared to a meteorite striking the earth. There are some large ones that produce deep craters. Meteor showers are more common, and although they usually disperse in the atmosphere, they can cause severe damage and consequences, both at the Earth's surface and inland. I thus found the coupling of trauma with ED difficult to understand and explain, until the metaphor of the meteorite gave me a helping hand: *the venomous ED can "touch, soften, soothe, relieve, and even restore sensation" to the epicentre where the meteorite or trauma fell.*

This coupling with ED generated a counterbalance, the illusion that it re-established a sense of proportion in psychic functioning. This process of articulation is characterised by approximation and coupling, even if it does not fit together at first, by being autonomous and very dynamic, in search of permanent tuning and better assembly. During this fine-tuning process, many elements generate noise. It is as if the meteorite has exposed swollen and infected areas that were previously undetectable to the naked eye. One of them is body image. When she was little, my daughter had no difficulties with her body that I can remember, though when she began overeating, the body change generated many painful comments focused on her physical appearance, with short and long term repercussions on her mental health. Ignorant comments from family members, both mine and my husband's, still weigh on her recovery.

A one-off comment from a stranger may not hurt as much, but one from someone the child has held in high esteem and affection carries a lot more weight. It is the inconsistency of giving love to the child with words, gifts, presence and listening and then, from the same loving source, using hurtful language in order to criticise the child's body through words, gestures, mockery and rejection. Many comments from loved ones that point equally at a developing girl's changing body and physique can therefore be devastating to her self-esteem and self-worth. Especially if the girl is highly sensitive, artistic, a perfectionist, independent and somewhat anxious.

Due to the effects of this inconsistency, my daughter began to report that she felt like a pig. As her intelligence led her to express it, she scanned what her family roots passed down through generations. It was the way we all looked at each other. I never really saw what she saw *in herself*, but I did see the weight of the animal on her slender shoulders.

Drawing 12: *Why Do I Feel like A Pig?* 2022

What I had to see was my critically anaemic daughter, faint, struggling skeletally between life and death to shake me. That is the reason why I embarked on a personal and family recovery, parallel to the unique and independent recovery and treatment of my daughter. My husband also undertook his own process. I continue to inquire and learn about the living reality of what can prevent mental suffering in a child, and how to give them the tools to discover their true beauty.

Ultimately, I hope that the question "Why my daughter?" (which at first seemed appropriate and now sounds somewhat absurd), will continue to help us pull back the veil and discover what might completely and definitively prevent the ED scaffolding anchored in my daughter for so long in generations to come.

How to break the binge eating-restriction cycle.

As I close the chapter on this intergenerational book of intake and bodily experience, I asked myself **how to get out** of this repetitive, unhealthy and silent cycle, one that leads us to oscillate between the impulse towards lightness, restriction as achievement and the completely opposite one that seeks caloric pleasure, comfort, accumulation at all costs, where we keep eating even though it hurts.

I begin to dream of a journey, rather like my grandfather Andres, on a raft with no food restrictions, no binge eating and no compensation. I lack a comfortable vessel and any credentials to man it, but I am adrift on a raft with only a pair of oars, and I am still afloat, with the joy of my own weight. It seems that I am on a raft whose stability among the waves is guaranteed only by the firmness of my body weight. Without this weight, the movement of the choppy sea and the lightness of the raft would definitely take me off course.

And there, in the middle of my living room, is the raft. Even when the waters are calm, there I am dealing with the ED demons that persist in deceiving and stealing my peace, the same insecurity in my face with indigenous features like those of my father Eusebio, my "bulging" stomach (as my mother Rosa Isabel described it), with an irreverent dinner that I like, very much in the Italian style of my mother-in-law Sarah, and all my emotions present. Fear is also in attendance, ensconced in its usual box.

By putting everything on the raft I have decided to continue to re-acquaint myself *from there*, and I refuse to give in to the obvious ED pandemic by doing nothing. I am learning from everything that happened in my own body and in my mind, striving to sort out and capture my experience in my drawings. I hope to successfully continue the task of bringing to light my changing relationship with the body and food by seeking reconciliation. I have been told several times by experts that if I stop restricting my eating, I will also stop triggering compulsive financial, emotional, academic or any other kind of binge-related behaviour, so I have put it to the test.

More than the result itself, the process has taught me to be aware of how to learn to eat without compensating via restriction or exercise. I have turned with compassion to my own body to connect with what it needs. I have recognised the need to stop "moralising" food, refusing to live as if there were good and *bad* or *forbidden* foods. To start eating without counting calories, portions, combinations and to feel free to do so at any time without imposing schedules on myself is something new for me. By daring, I have found that I am healthier if I listen to my own body. Tuning into my own body and spiritual frequency is more necessary than following and being alerted to the latest nutritional breakthroughs on Instagram or Facebook. I resolve not to live in vigilance as to how many daily steps I have achieved and whether I have reached the minimum 3,000 or 10,000 steps, or 4 to 8 glasses of water daily, as dictated by the internet as healthy for all human beings regardless of our physical composition, activity levels or medical history.

In doing so, I seek nothing more than a personal re-understanding of what food is, what the body is, what health and ultimately life itself is all about, and I will not give up even if I have to row against a fantasy ideal of healthy eating and a dwarfed and invisible body. All food groups (vegetables, fruits, grains, proteins, fats, carbohydrates, etc.) are rich in nutrients necessary for the proper functioning of my own and my family's bodies and minds. As for exercise, I want to find it fun and choose to rest when my body asks me to. Exercise should not be a form of punishment or atonement. If we avoid (conscientiously, in this case) comparisons of physical attributes and characteristics, we will begin to understand the wonder that each person is unique and unrepeatable in their mind, body, experiences, emotions and ultimately their spirit, however we understand it. That is true respect for the self.

What I have received by managing to enter a phase of recovery does not compare to the person I have become as a result of starting the process. And during all this, my daughter has begun to show signs of a personal and sustained recovery of her own. My daughter is undoubtedly on her own raft; she knows I am there for as long as she needs me. However, I make sure that I always keep moving forward on my own raft. There are stops that reveal themselves as rests, others as recharges, suddenly turning to go back, to connect, feel, understand, learn and draw. Free of any value judgements. I move forward because it is who I am. I am at peace with my own pace and my own journey. Many times, my raft even drifts away from my daughter's raft. My raft is my world;

there, with my body, I examine my responsibilities one by one, and my legacy as I pass through this world; they let me move forward, whether the sea is rough or not. It is there that I connect with my emotions, with myself and with God. This is where I can draw and blur my present in order to untangle and connect myself, and thus continue drawing my reality.

By recognising the freedom to experience my body from another perspective, I can see the horizon of acceptance. Approaching eating as an act of service to myself, I repay the debt I had been carrying for the disservice I did to my own body, my mind, my whole being. In doing so, I seek to reinvent my relationship with the tight clothing button, with the mirror and the perspective of my plate, with the morsel in my mouth. Only now—and after many years—I am beginning to broaden my perception of myself. I have left behind the fantasy of becoming a small, chiselled and sculpted body, with a flat belly, bulging musculature at the point of low-calorie bites, counted one by one obsessively.

Yes, sometimes I have encountered the past, my grandmother Sofia, in the prison of her despair, as I despair and I accept it; I have also encountered my father Eusebio, always generous to others. I choose to borrow from his generosity and continue to treat myself equally, without judgement or blame. I have also seen my mother Rosa Isabel again, seeking to improve herself in some way, seeking to belong to a group that makes her feel that she is "progressing". As I navigate the intergenerational floodways, I connect with thousands of mistreatments and sufferings, restrictions and excesses that were part of my enslaving past and that, by the same token, now deserve my full attention. The attention I give is not given as a victim or as a survivor but as someone seeking a path of growth, of self-awareness of compassion for self and others.

My new life encourages me to make up my mind and break the generational lines of guilt and pretension, severity and rigidity of being; that "should be" that puts *the glimpse of the other* before true priorities. Today I am breaking with the conventionalism that taught me that certain dress sizes are more desirable than others. That there are rules about who can wear a figure-hugging suit and who can go to the beach in a swimming costume and jump in the water on a sweltering day. Today I want and I choose to break the shadows of what is transmitted about what is disgusting and what is unthinkable with regard to women, food and weight. Weight weighs nothing. When one is better nourished, better connected with himself or herself, better accompanied, who walks in peace, will no doubt get there sooner. I want to strut around with the body I have, with the wrinkles that appear, like someone wearing a designer suit. I allow myself to savour the taste of food and life without shame or guilt. I want to savour the fervent desire to live well, without punishment or threats. It is the only way to start a new intergenerational line based on care, respect, validation and humanity.

Drawing 13: *I Care For You*, 2022

I have finally begun to discover what helps my daughter in her process at home and in my relationship with her, the mum she needs and the mum she doesn't, even though it is a dynamic, ever-changing process. This same determination encourages me to keep on inquiring, since she is constantly transforming, growing, maturing and progressing. Today, I know one thing: she needs me **free**.

Today I draw myself in freedom.

Drawing 14: *Daring To Be*, 2022

THE END

References

1) MacNeill, L.P., Best, L.A. & Davis, L.L. The role of personality in body image dissatisfaction and disordered eating: discrepancies between men and women. Journal of Eating Disorders, 5, 44 (2017). *https://dio.org/10.1186/s40337-017-0177-8*

2) Deloitte Access Economics. The Social and Economic Cost of Eating Disorders in the United States of America: A Report for the Strategic Training Initiative for the Prevention of Eating Disorders and the Academy for Eating Disorders. June 2020. Available at: Report: Economic Costs of Eating Disorders